Wellbeing for kids

Making kids smarter, happier

STAGES 1-3

Kate Daniels & Victoria Pugh

HC CB
HARPERCOLLINS CHILDREN'S BOOKS

First published by Collins
This edition published in India in 2024 by HarperCollins *Children's Books*
An imprint of HarperCollins *Publishers* India
Building No 10, Tower A, 4th Floor, DLF Cyber City, Phase II,
Gurugram – 122002

2 4 6 8 10 9 7 5 3 1

P-ISBN: 978-93-6569-274-7

William Collins' dream of knowledge for all began with the publication of his first book in 1819.
A self-educated mill worker, he not only enriched millions of lives, but also founded a flourishing publishing house. Today, staying true to this spirit, Collins books are packed with inspiration, innovation and practical expertise.
They place you at the centre of a world of possibility and give you exactly what you need to explore it.
Collins. Freedom to teach.

Series editor: Kate Daniels
Author: Victoria Pugh
Publisher: Elaine Higgleton
Author of the introduction: Becky Goddard-Hill
Product developer: Roisin Leahy
Development and copy editor: Jo Kemp
Proofreader: Claire Throp

Illustrations by Jouve India Ltd.
Cover design by Shamika Chaves

Typeset by Sam Vail, Ken Vail Graphic Design

Printed and bound at Nutech Print Services - India

HarperCollinsIn

Contents

Contents

Stage 2

Contents

Stage 3

LETTER TO PARENTS/GUARDIAN

Dear parent or guardian,

Welcome to the Collins International Wellbeing course, and the start of your child's wellbeing journey.

Collins supports this learning journey for your child through the materials in this course, and we'd like you, as parents/guardians, to be part of the experience. This letter explains how the course works, and how you can help your child to get the maximum benefit from the Collins materials.

What is the Collins Wellbeing course?

Concerns around the wellbeing of children have grown since the Covid-19 pandemic; children might have spent more time at home during the pandemic than they otherwise would have, and this has had an impact on the development of children's language and social skills, and sense of self. The Collins Wellbeing materials have been written to support parents/guardians who need to help their children navigate a world that may be unfamiliar to them, and to help support young children who need help developing their social skills, and who may be more anxious about social interactions than children used to be.

Children learn most in the first five years of life: the early years and time spent in kindergarten and nursery are recognised as the essential foundations for success at school. Millions of children will have missed out on essential formative experiences in nurseries and kindergartens because of the pandemic, and schools are now having to help children catch up. Gaps in learning – caused in this instance by the pandemic – are being recognised widely; there are similar gaps in the emotional and personal development of young children. The Collins Wellbeing course has been designed to help ensure that children are fully supported in terms of their social, personal and emotional development.

Similarly, the secondary course has been designed to support older children who have had big gaps in their social experiences of school and relationships with peers, due to the pandemic, at a formative time in their development. Our research with teachers has particularly highlighted increased anxiety in older students, especially around things like giving presentations in school, and how they manage their feelings of anxiety in different settings, and the course has been designed specifically to support that.

There is a large body of research that highlights the important benefits for children's future and achievements of focusing on wellbeing. Research suggests strong links between student wellbeing and improved academic achievement (Kirkcaldy et al., 2004; Suldo et al., 2011), while incidents of academic underachievement are associated with poorer student wellbeing (van Batenburg-Eddes & Jolles, 2013).

Other characteristics such as self-confidence and growth mindset, both of which are important for academic success, have been linked with higher student wellbeing (King, 2017), and students with lower wellbeing have been found to be at a greater risk of behavioural difficulties and school drop-out compared to their peers with higher levels of wellbeing (Arslan & Renshaw, 2018).

As such, we hope you'll agree that it is essential to support your child's wellbeing effectively.

The Covid pandemic is just one example of an event that has caused gaps in learning; this course aims to provide your children with the tools and resilience required to cope well in a range of scenarios.

Being involved as a parent/guardian

There is nothing covered in this course that should raise concerns for you. Topics covered include: identifying and managing emotions; developing healthy habits; establishing healthy relationships with peers, and how to cope when these change; being a part of a community; how to stay safe in school, at home and online; how to cope with change; and how to live sustainably and ethically.

The book that your child will be using is a workbook that they can write into, and can be used as a record of the topics they have covered, as well as something that they can refer back to in order to recap things they have learned to support their wellbeing.

Using this resource

While most of the lessons in the book will require some amount of engagement and intervention from you as the parent/guardian and will be self explanatory, there are a few chapters that will require you to be more hands-on and organize activities to drive the lesson home. Please scan this QR code to access the Wellbeing Parents' Guide, which will have detailed activities as well as lesson plans for your child.

We hope you make the most of this resource and encourage the wellbeing of your child.

Harper Collins Team

Wellbeing for kids

Making kids smarter, happier

STAGE 1

Hello and welcome to Wellbeing Stage 1!

Let's take a quick look at what is inside.

Feelings

Starting school can be exciting! But you might feel lots of other different things too, like feeling shy or scared or worried. Because you are in a classroom with lots of other children it is important to understand their feelings too. This book will help you understand more about both your feelings and those of other people.

Understanding yourself

The activities in your book will help you find out what makes you happy or sad and what helps you if you are feeling angry or upset. There is a lot you can do to help yourself feel better.

Being healthy

Being healthy is very important, so we will look at exercise, eating well and teeth brushing in this section!

Family and friends

Getting on well with other people at home and in the classroom is important too because it helps us be happy. So we are going to have a look at how to do this too.

Keeping safe

Learning to look after yourself in school and when you are outside will keep you safe. And working through these workbooks will help!

Growing up

You are growing up and starting school is a big step towards growing up. Let's look at what growing up means.

Being special

Finally, we are going to take a look at what makes you special. Because you are special!

I hope you enjoy your wellbeing book.

May your year be as wonderful as you are!

– *Becky Goddard-Hill*

Unit 1.1 How do I feel?

What do you know?

- What can you see in the picture?
- Can you tick the emojis that show feelings you have felt at some time?

In this unit, you will:

- Create emotion stones.
- Think of ways to help a friend when they are experiencing big emotions.
- Explore what empathy means.

Lesson 1 My feelings

Activity 1.1a My feelings

What makes you feel happy, sad and excited? Write your answers below and say why these things make you feel this way.

I feel happy when ______________________________

____

because ______________________________

____

I feel sad when ______________________________

____

because ______________________________

____

I feel excited when ______________________________

____

because ______________________________

____

Lesson 1 My feelings

Activity 1.1b When I feel angry

Draw or write things you could do to calm yourself down when you feel angry.

Lesson 1 My feelings

Activity 1.1c Emotion stones

Decorate each pebble with a different emotion. Think about the shapes, colours and how they would feel to hold. Rough or smooth? Heavy or light? Discuss your choices with your parents/guardians and friends.

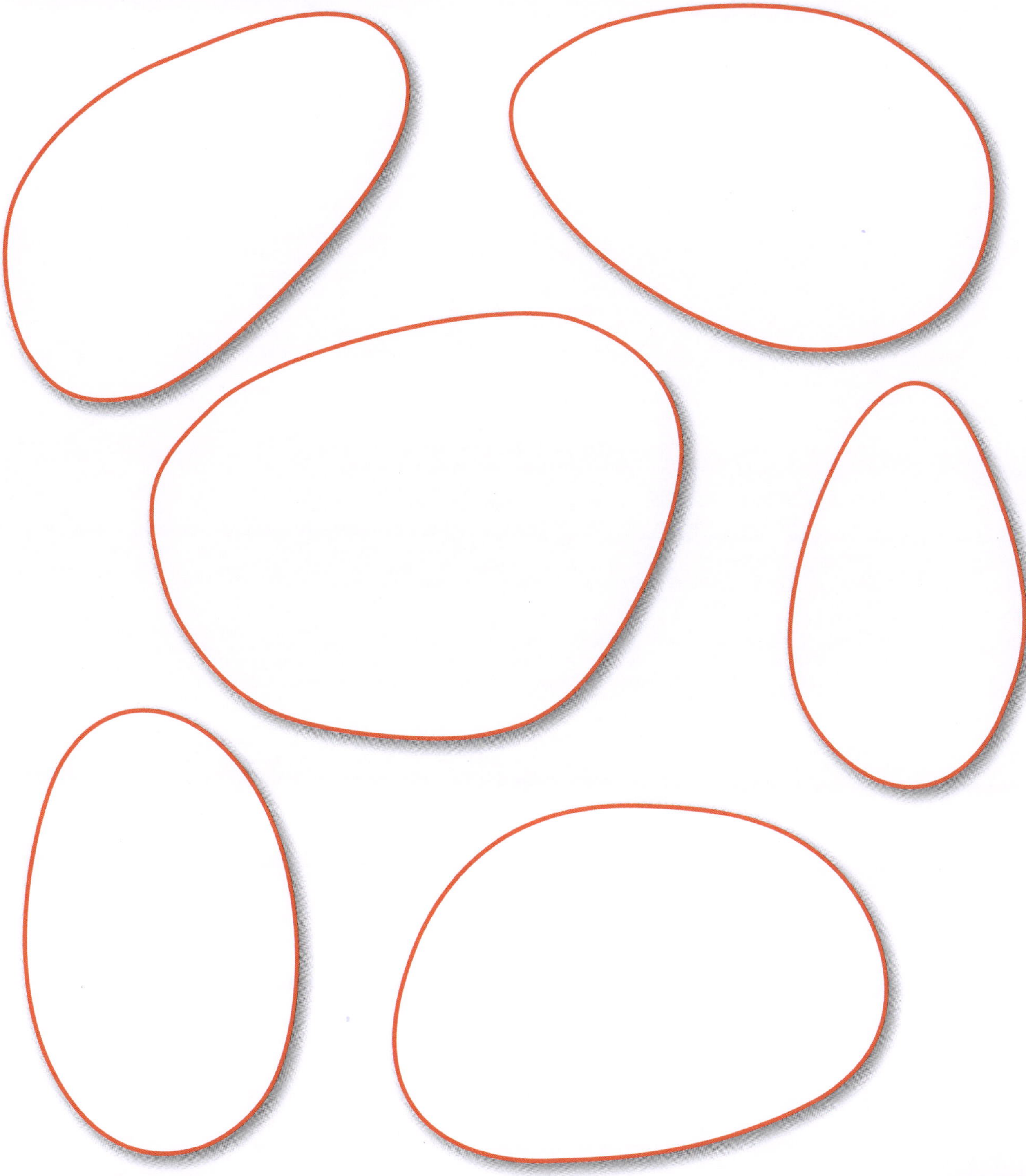

Lesson 2 Other people's feelings

Activity 1.2a What is empathy?

When we are able to understand what someone is feeling, or be mindful of others' emotions, that is empathy. Can you draw some pictures to show what empathy is?

What is empathy?

Lesson 2 Other people's feelings

Activity 1.2b How can I help?

If your friend is upset or in trouble, how could you help them?

Lesson 3 It's OK to feel this way

Activity 1.3 Reflection

Can you name all of the emotions below? Why do you think such an emotion would arise?

Unit reflection

Can you match the emotion words to the photos? Draw a line from the emotion picture to the matching emotion word.

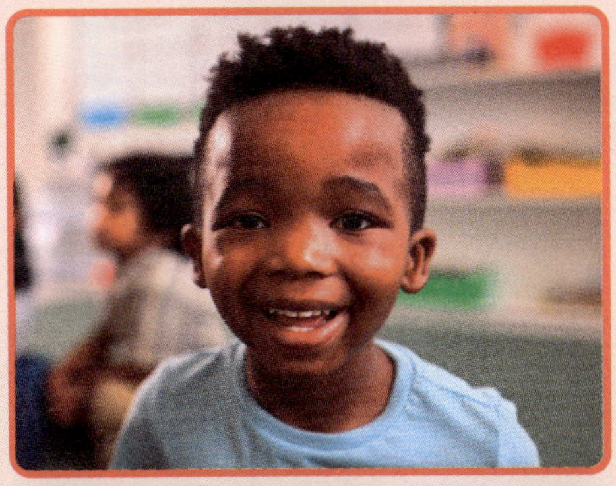

Excited

Happy

Sad

Shocked

Unit 1.2 Exploring my emotions

What do you know?

- What can you see in the pictures? Can you name the different emotions present?
- Circle the faces which you think show happiness in yellow and circle the faces which you think show sadness in blue.

In this unit, you will:

- Explore what makes you feel happy and sad.
- Tackle some problem-solving challenges.

Lesson 1 What makes me happy or sad?

Activity 2.1a Happy collage

Create your own happy collage. Cut out pictures from magazines, photos or shapes to create your collage.

Lesson 1 What makes me happy or sad?

Activity 2.1b What makes me happy or sad?

In the circles below, write or draw things which make you happy or sad. Remember, if you are ever feeling sad you can talk to your friends, family and your trusted adults.

Lesson 2 Don't give up!

Activity 2.2a Animal sudoku

Fill the missing boxes by drawing either a teddy bear, a cat, a horse or a mouse to complete your sudoku puzzle. Remember, each animal should only appear once in each column, row and block.

Lesson 2 Don't give up!

Activity 2.2b Problem-solving challenges

Can you complete these challenges?

- Can you complete a jigsaw? ☐
- Can you make a bridge using construction blocks? ☐
- Can you write as many words as you can think of beginning with the letter 'b'? ☐
- Can you design a new game to play? ☐
- Can you make up a joke to tell? ☐

Lesson 3 I am unique

Activity 2.3a Things I like

Draw a picture of yourself in the box in the middle and all of the things you like in the circles.

Me!

Lesson 3 I am unique

Activity 2.3b I am so special!

List three things which make you special. Once you're done, ask your parents/guardian the same question.

1. ______________________________

2. ______________________________

3. ______________________________

Unit reflection

Colour in the flower using your favourite colours. In the centre of the flower, draw or write some things that you can do to help yourself feel better if you feel sad, want to give up or are feeling some big emotions.

Unit 1.3 Looking after myself

What do you know?

- What can you see in the pictures?
- Can you name each of the foods?
- What foods do you enjoy?
- Are there any foods you don't enjoy as much?

In this unit, you will:

- Explore what foods are good for our bodies.
- Learn how to brush your teeth correctly.

Lesson 1 Healthy food habits

Activity 3.1a Favourite meal picture

Create a picture of your favourite meal. Ask your friends what their favourite meals are. Do any of them sound delicious? Would you like to try them?

My favourite meal is ______________________________

____

____

Lesson 1 Healthy food habits

Activity 3.1b Fruit rockets

What kinds of fruits can go together? Use your imagination and create fruit rockets, with pieces of fruits connected to each other with a skewer to look like a rocket. What fruit did you use? What shape was each piece? What colour was each piece of fruit?

Label each fruit rocket.

Lesson 2 Moving and shaking

Activity 3.2a Exercise

What are your favourite ways to exercise?

Draw pictures in the shapes below.

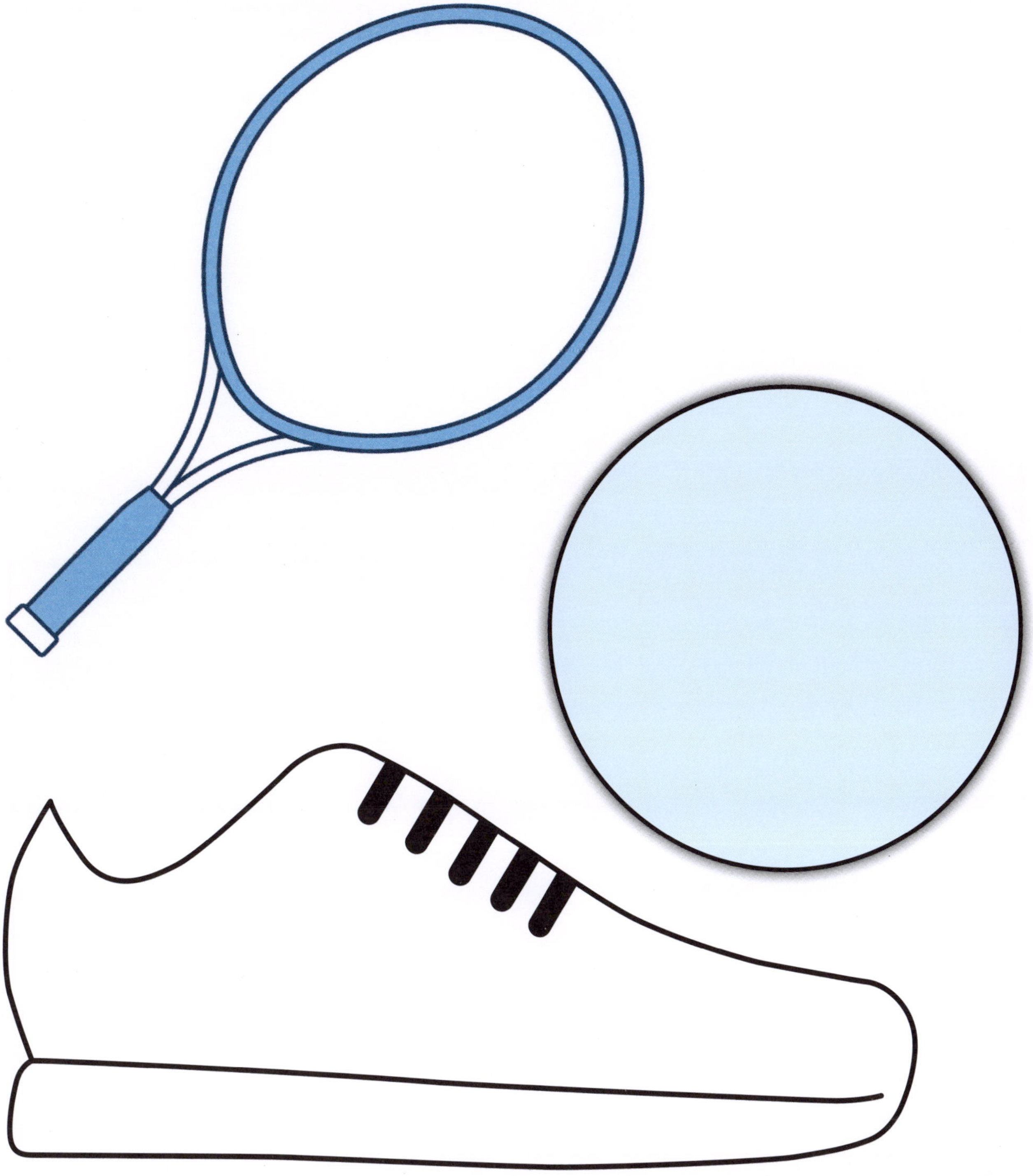

Lesson 2 Moving and shaking

Activity 3.2b I would like to try...

Think about any new sports or movement you would like to try. Draw them below.

Lesson 3 Brush your teeth

Activity 3.3a How should I brush my teeth?

Think about the things you need to do when brushing your teeth properly.
Draw each stage in the boxes below.

Lesson 3 Brush your teeth

Activity 3.3b The teeth-brushing song

Illustrate the words to the teeth-brushing song. What pictures could you draw to show what to do when you brush your teeth?

This is the way we brush our teeth,
brush our teeth, brush our teeth.
This is the way we brush our teeth,
early in the morning.

We brush our teeth from side to
side, side to side, side to side.
We brush our teeth from side to
side, so they are nice and clean.

We brush our teeth up and down, up
and down, up and down.
We brush our teeth up and down, so
they are nice and clean.

This is the way we brush our teeth,
brush our teeth, brush our teeth.
This is the way we brush our teeth,
before we go to bed.

Unit reflection

In this unit we have been learning about healthy meals, exercise and keeping our teeth clean. Think about the things you have learned and draw or write what you remember below.

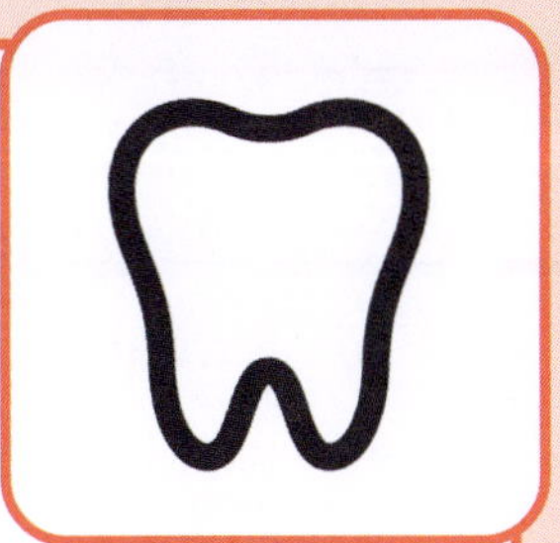

Unit 1.4 People who are special to me

I'm Glad I'm Me

No one looks the way I do,
I have noticed that it's true.
No one walks the way I walk.
No one talks the way I talk.
No one plays the way I play
No one says the things I say.
I am special,
I am Me.
There is no one I would
Rather be
Than Me!

By Jack Prelutsky

What do you know?

- What do you think the poem is about?
- What makes you special?
- Are we all different?

In this unit, you will:

- Draw a comic strip to show a special day in your life.
- Create a friendship bracelet for a friend.
- Explore the ways we can make friends.

Lesson 1 People who love me

Activity 4.1a What we do together

Draw a picture of what activities you like to do with people you love. This might be a picture of somewhere you have been together or an activity you like to share.

Lesson 1 People who love me

Activity 4.1b A special day

Think of a special day that you have spent with someone you love. Draw a comic strip below of what you did.

Lesson 2 We are all the same, we are all different

Activity 4.2a Family celebrations

Draw a picture or make a collage of your family celebrating a special event, day or time in your life.

Lesson 2 We are all the same, we are all different

Activity 4.2b Is it ok to be different?

Look at the sentences below. Do you agree or disagree with them? If you agree, draw a smiley face in the box. If you disagree, draw a sad face in the box. After you're done, ask your family members the same questions.

	Agree or disagree?
If people are different, they can't be friends.	
Being friends with someone who is different from you is interesting as you can learn about someone else's life.	
You should be unkind to people if they are different from you.	
You don't have to agree with your friends all the time.	

Lesson 3 Making friends

Activity 4.3a Friend story

Can you act out the story below with your friends?

What do you think is happening in each of the pictures? How do you think the story ends?

Lesson 3 Making friends

Activity 4.3b Friendship bracelet

Can you design a friendship bracelet for your friend?

What are their favourite colours and patterns?

Draw your design below.

Unit reflection

Think of someone who is your friend.

What do you like to do together?

How do they make you feel? How do you know they are your friend?

Draw or write your answers below.

How my friend makes me feel

How I like to spend time with my friend

How I know they are my friend

Unit 1.5 Working together

What do you know?

- What is happening in the photo?
- Who is joining in?
- Do you think they know each other?

In this unit, you will:

- Explore ways to make up with friends if you have fallen out.
- Look at a range of communities and share what communities you belong to.
- Agree on some rules for your room and home.

Lesson 1 Falling out

Activity 5.1 Me apologising

Think of a time when you have apologised. Why did you need to apologise? And who did you apologise to? Draw a picture of you apologising. What happened after you apologised?

Which words did you use to apologise?

sorry forgive because apologise
felt sad friend

Lesson 2 Our community

Activity 5.2a Our community project

Design a project which can help people in your neighbourhood. Think about these questions.

Who would you like to help?

____

How could you help the community?

____

____

What might your project look like? Draw a picture of it below.

Lesson 2 Our community

Activity 5.2b What is community?

What do you think about when you hear the word 'community'? What does it mean? What communities do you belong to?

Community

Lesson 3 Rules rule!

Activity 5.3a Silly rules

What silly rules do you think might be fun to try out?

Remember, your rule must be silly but not something that could cause someone to get hurt.

Draw a poster to show your silly rule below.

Lesson 3 Rules rule!

Activity 5.3b A super classmate

What makes a super classmate? What do they do that makes them so great?

Draw a picture of your super classmate and all the things they do below.

Lesson 3 Rules rule!

Activity 5.3c My class rule book

Draw the rules of your classroom below. Talk to your parents/guardian about why each rule is important.

You can write the rule below your drawing if you would like to.

Unit reflection

Create your own school

If you started your own school, what rules would you have? Think about rules that keep us safe, happy and kind.

My school rules

1. ______________________________

2. ______________________________

3. ______________________________

Unit 1.6 Keeping myself safe

What do you know?

- What can you see in the picture?
- What are all of these things for?
- Who might use these items?

In this unit, you will:

- Learn why rules in the classroom are important.
- Explore ways to keep safe in your home.
- Learn about keeping your personal information safe online.

Lesson 1 Staying safe in school

Activity 6.1 Portrait gallery

Think about the people who keep you safe in school. Draw a picture of adults in school who help to keep you safe.

Lesson 2 Road safety

Activity 6.2a How do you get to school?

Can you create a pictogram to show how children in your class get to school? Use icons of various vehicles (car, bike, bicycle, bus, etc.) to portray different transports, with each icon standing for one student. So, if four students get to class by bus, add four bus icons. See which is the most common transport. Which kind of transport requires a lot of precautions?

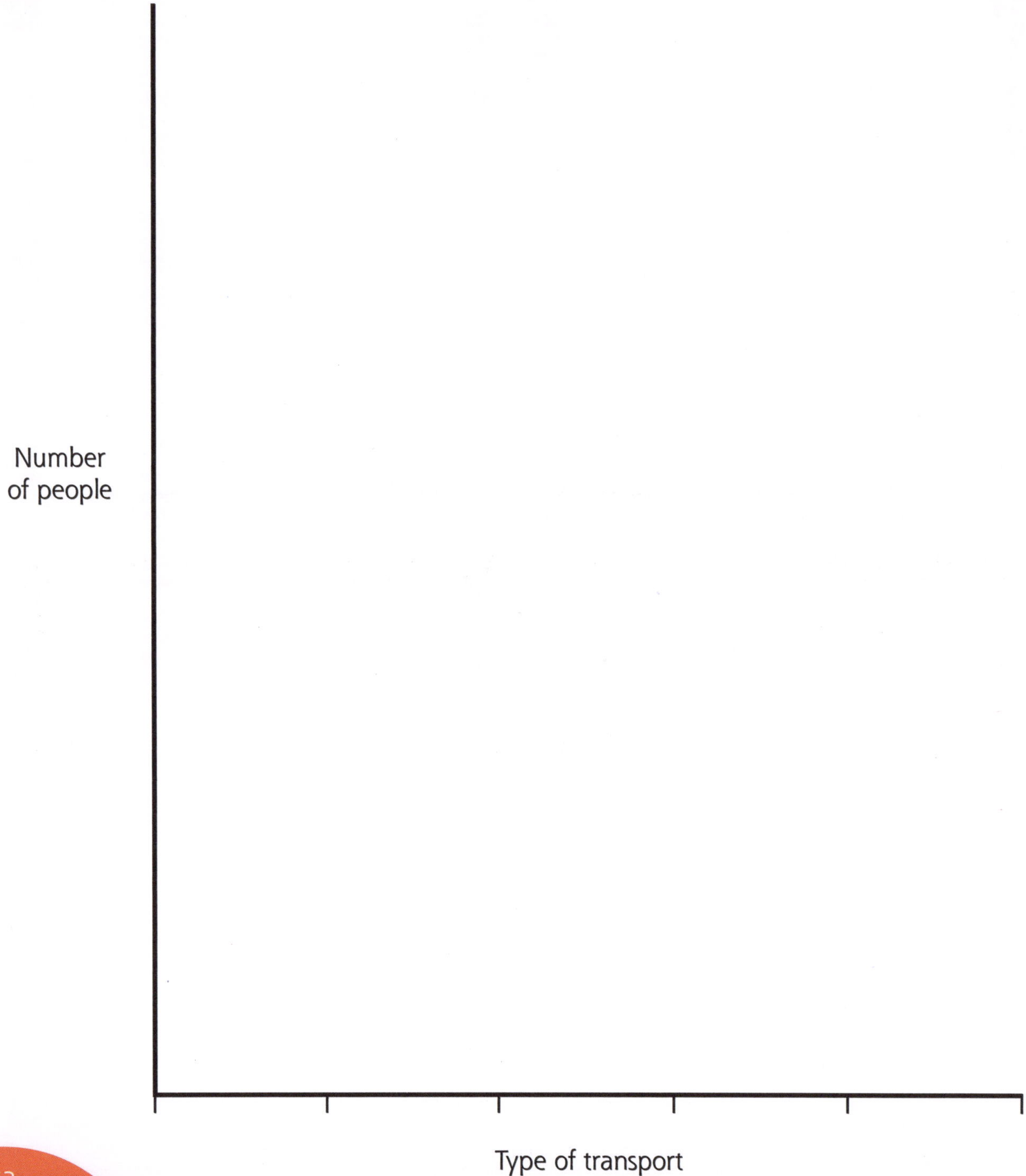

Lesson 2 Road safety

Activity 6.2b Different types of transport

Draw a picture of a type of transport. You might like to draw a car, train, aeroplane or tram. Think of the transport you take every week.

Lesson 3 Do I know you?

Activity 6.3a What would you share?

What information would you share with a stranger?

Would you share ...	Yes	No
Your name?		
Your address?		
Your favourite colour?		
The name of your school?		
Your favourite toy?		
Where you have been on holiday?		

Lesson 3 Do I know you?

Activity 6.3b Devices are great

What games or apps do you like to play on your devices? Draw your favourite games below and write what makes them so fun to play.

Lesson 3 Do I know you?

Activity 6.3c Top tips

What are your top tips for staying safe online? Draw your top three tips. Ask your family members about their tips to stay safe online.

Unit reflection

Discuss with your friend whether the people in the pictures are safe.
Could they do anything different to be safer?

Unit 1.7 I am growing up

What do you know?

- What can you see in the picture?
- What do you think is happening?
- Where do you think you are in the picture?

In this unit, you will:

- Order the life cycle of a human.
- Create 'I can' posters to show all of the things you can do now and would like to do in the future.
- Explore how it feels to move to a different class or year group.

Lesson 1 I am growing

Activity 7.1a Human life cycle

Cut out the pictures from the worksheet shared by your parent/guardian. Stick them below in order from youngest to oldest.

Lesson 1 I am growing

Activity 7.1b Time travel scrapbook

Think of the changes that have happened in your life. How did they make you feel?

Draw or write about the changes you have experienced below and how they made you feel. You can start your time travel scrapbook from when you were a baby.

Lesson 2 Being independent

Activity 7.2 I can

Get your parent/guardian to write on small bits of paper things that an independent person can do. Put them in a box. Draw randomly from the box and write whether you can do the task on your own. How confident do you feel that you can do each task? Draw an emoji in the box to show how confident you feel about each task.

	I can ...
	I can ...
	I can ...
	I can ...
	I can ...

Lesson 3 Moving on up

Activity 7.3a I am proud

I am proud of

because

Lesson 3 Moving on up

Activity 7.3b My new class wish

My wish for my new class is ______________________________

Lesson 3 Moving on up

Activity 7.3c Tomas's first day

Look at the pictures of Tomas's first day in the purple class. Talk to your friend or parent/guardian about what is happening in each picture.

How do you think Tomas felt after his first day?

Unit reflection

It's time to reflect on growing up and all the exciting changes that will happen in your life. We know that we can prepare for changes by asking questions, asking for help if we need it and by remembering that it's ok to make mistakes and try again.

Think about the things you are looking forward to as you get older. What are the top three things you are looking forward to as you become more independent?

1. ______________________________

2. ______________________________

3. ______________________________

Unit 1.8 Celebrating difference

What do you know?

- What can you see in the pictures?
- Circle the foods you enjoy and put a cross beside the foods you dislike.

In this unit, you will:

- Find out how chocolate is made and even try some!
- Explore different celebrations and find out what events and occasions your friends celebrate.
- Create friendship bracelets for your friends.

Lesson 1 Where does my food come from?

Activity 8.1a How is chocolate made?

Can you put the pictures in order? Put the number 1 in the box to show which photo is the first in the sequence, then 2 in the second one and so on. Find out where the various ingredients of chocolate come from, and where it gets made.

Lesson 1 Where does my food come from?

Activity 8.1b My favourite chocolate

Do you like chocolate?

Draw a picture of your favourite chocolate bar or sweet treat.

Lesson 2 What do you celebrate?

Activity 8.2a What do you like to celebrate?

Draw pictures of the events you like to celebrate. What is your favourite part of the celebrations?

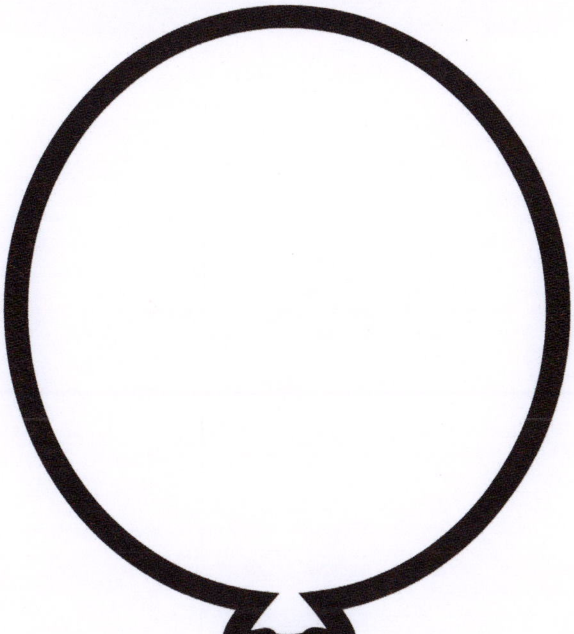

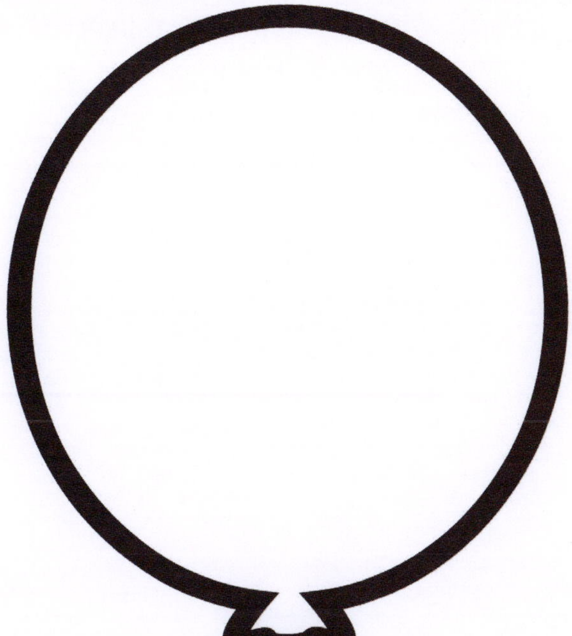

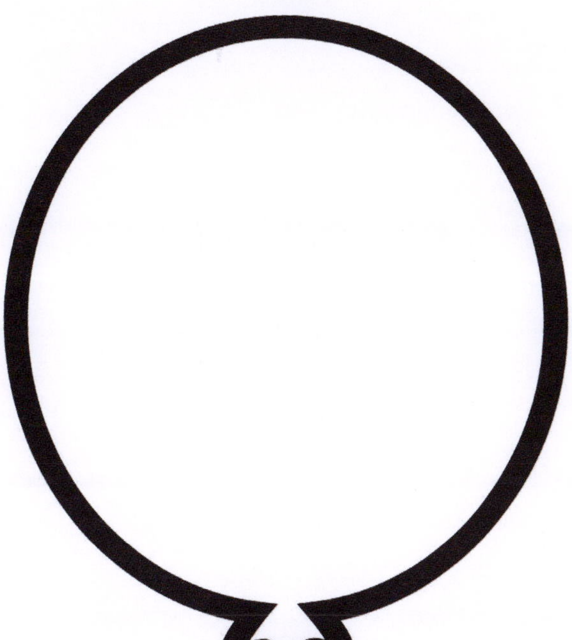

Lesson 2 What do you celebrate?

Activity 8.2b Party time planning

Think about a time when you have celebrated or have been to a party. What decorations or things did you see there?

Imagine you are planning a party. Draw all of the things you might need or the decorations you might design.

Lesson 3 We are all different

Activity 8.3a Similarities and differences

Answer the questions below, then ask a friend the same questions. If any answers are the same, circle them in blue; if any are different, circle them in green. You can write some of your own questions as well.

	My answer	**My friend's answer**
What is your favourite colour?		
If you could have any superpower, what would it be?		
What is your favourite way to help people?		
What is your favourite thing about school?		
What is your favourite book or story?		

Lesson 3 We are all different

Activity 8.3b What have you learned?

Can you complete the sentence below?

It is great to be different because

Unit reflection

Draw a picture of your favourite celebration food.

What makes it special and different from the food you eat every day?

Where do you think the ingredients to make this food come from?

Wellbeing for kids

Making kids smarter, happier

STAGE 2

Hello and welcome to Wellbeing Stage 2!

Emotions

It can really help to understand your feelings. In this book we are going to look at ways to help you when you feel angry. And we are going to find things that make you feel happy.

Health

Keeping your mind feeling healthy is really important and that is the main reason for this book. It's important to look at how to keep your body healthy too, so you feel fantastic inside and out.

Friendships

Friendships are brilliant but not if you feel left out. So it's important to know how to make everyone feel included. We also need to learn what to do when we fall out with our friends or if someone is being unkind. Being a good friend really matters, so let's look at how to do this.

Emergencies

Can you recognise dangers at home and school? We are going to explore how to keep safe.

The future

Thinking about changes that can happen in the future can be super exciting. I wonder what job you will do!

How might you make the world a better place? There are lots of ways!

Are you ready to start thinking about how to look after yourself, other people and the planet?

Let's go for it!

May your year be as amazing as you!

Becky Goddard-Hill

Unit 2.1 My feelings

What do you know?

- What can you see in the pictures?
- What emotions might each of the characters be feeling?
- Share a time when you have felt an emotion like this.

In this unit, you will:

- Explore how your body reacts to different emotions.
- How emotions can make us behave in different ways.

Lesson 1 What are feelings?

Activity 1.1 Emotion words

What emotion words do you know? What do you think is the difference between emotion and feeling? List them below, or you could draw emojis to show each emotion and label it.

Lesson 2 Emotions and behaviour

Activity 1.2a An argument

Umair and Cara are cousins and they play together every weekend when their mums are playing hockey. One day, they are playing a board game when Umair gets cross. He thinks Cara is cheating and starts to push her to stop her having another turn. She tells him she isn't cheating and that these are the rules, but he doesn't agree. Umair tips up the board game, knocking everything over, and runs out of the room. Cara starts to cry.

How does Umair feel?

____

____

____

How does Cara feel?

____

____

____

Lesson 2 Emotions and behaviour

Activity 1.2b Action time!

Two friends, Ellie and Suraj are sitting together in class. Suraj is finding the maths problems very difficult, while Ellie finds them easy and is already on to the next page of the exercise book. Suraj wants to ask for Ellie's help, but he also doesn't want to bother her. Act out the scenario as described and try acting out how it ends as well. Stop at key points in the story to take a picture or draw the important parts of the story in the storyboard below. How does the story end?

Write a sentence to describe each part of the story.

1. ______________________________

2. ______________________________

3. ______________________________

4. ______________________________

Lesson 3 Feeling great!

Activity 1.3a What makes you feel happy?

Draw in the shapes what you like to do that helps you feel happy.

Lesson 3 Feeling great!

Activity 1.3b What would you like to do more of to make you happy?

Draw some examples of things which you would like to do more of to make you happy.

Unit reflection

If you are feeling in a bad mood, how might you act?

What could you do to help yourself feel better? Draw your ideas in the boxes.

Unit 2.2 My marvellous mind

BE CREATIVE

EXERCISE

HYDRATE

EAT HEALTHILY

What do you know?

- What do each of the pictures show?
- When do you do each of these things?
- Do you think these things are important to do each day? Why?

In this unit, you will:

- Explore why it is important to look after our minds.
- Try out different relaxation and self-care activities.
- Think about what characters can do to feel better in different situations.

Lesson 1 Marvellous minds

Activity 2.1 Journal page

As you go through the unit, write down any new words you come across. You can use a dictionary to find out what each word means and then put the definition into your own words. You can also use this page to jot down any ideas or thoughts you have throughout the unit about self-care and big emotions.

Lesson 2 Self-care and relaxation

Activity 2.2 Take your pencil for a walk!

Listen to relaxing music and just draw. It doesn't have to be a picture or a shape we can recognise. You can use squiggly lines or circles, anything you like. You can use the shapes to doodle in, or use the rest of the page, or both.

Lesson 3 Big emotions

Activity 2.3 Big emotion scenarios

Once upon a time, there was a boy named Max who received some fantastic news – he found out that his best friend was going to sleep over at his house. Max couldn't contain his excitement and started talking really loudly and quickly. He shouted and ran around, jumping up and down and spinning around in circles.

In all the excitement, Max accidentally knocked over a lamp and it smashed. It was an accident, but he realised that his big feelings were affecting his behaviour.

What could Max do to calm himself down? Discuss with your parents/guardians and make notes below.

Once upon a time, there was a girl named Aisha who woke up feeling really grumpy one morning. She didn't know why, but everything seemed to irritate her. The sun was too bright, the birds were too loud and even her favourite cereal tasted different.

Aisha's grumpiness followed her throughout the day. When her mum asked her to tidy her room, she stomped her feet and crossed her arms, saying, "I don't want to!" Her little brother tried to play with her, but she snapped at him, telling him to leave her alone.

As the day went on, Aisha's grumpiness grew bigger and bigger. She realised that her feelings were affecting how she treated others. It made her sad to see her family upset because of her grumpiness.

What could Aisha do? What can you do to stop yourself feeling grumpy? Ask your family members and make notes below.

Once upon a time, in a bustling city, there lived a curious boy named Hassan. Hassan loved exploring the world around him and was always eager to learn new things. One sunny day, Hassan woke up feeling a little anxious. He couldn't quite explain why, but his tummy felt fluttery, and his hands were sweaty. As he got ready for school, the feeling of anxiety grew stronger, and he began to worry about what the day would bring.

As Hassan arrived at school, he noticed a new student sitting alone. His name was Omar, and he looked nervous and unsure. Hassan couldn't bear to see someone feeling lonely, so he mustered up his courage and approached him.

"Hi, I'm Hassan. Would you like to be friends?" he asked with a warm smile. Omar looked up, his eyes filled with relief, and nodded shyly.

How might Omar feel? Write the rest of the story below.

Unit reflection

What types of big feelings might people feel in their lives? Look back at your notes on your journal page for Activity 2.1.

What can you do to manage your big emotions if they aren't making you feel good? What can you do to make yourself or others feel better?

Unit 2.3 Staying healthy

What do you know?

- What does being healthy mean?
- How do you keep healthy?
- What can you see in each picture?

In this unit, you will:

- Complete a survey to find out all the things that students in your school do to keep healthy.
- Create your own healthy lifestyle plans.
- Take part in experiments to see how you can stop germs spreading.

Lesson 1 Things that keep us healthy

Activity 3.1a Health survey

Conduct a health survey at your school. Go into each class, remembering to knock on the door. Tell the class what you are doing, then ask the questions below. Ask their teacher to help if you need to. Say thank you and go back to your class.

Activity	Tally
Do you walk to school?	
Do you cycle to school?	
Do you play outside?	
Do you do a sport or other club?	
Do you do any other exercise?	
Do you like exercise?	
Total of tally marks:	

Lesson 1 Things that keep us healthy

Activity 3.1b Making healthy changes

Think of all the changes you could make, or the healthy choices you make in your day. Write or draw them in the bubbles below.

Lesson 2 Keeping fit is fun

Activity 3.2a My favourite exercise

How do you like to exercise?

Draw a picture below of you taking part in your favourite activity which helps to keep you fit and healthy.

Lesson 2 Keeping fit is fun

Activity 3.2b My fitness journal

What exercise do you take part in over the week? Remember that exercise can be any type of activity where you are moving your body, such as stretching, games, yoga or team sports.

	Type of exercise	How did it make you feel?
Monday		
Tuesday		
Wednesday		
Thursday		
Friday		
Saturday		
Sunday		

Lesson 3 Germs, germs, germs

Activity 3.3a When should we wash our hands?

Think about times when we should wash our hands.
Write four examples below.

1. ______________________________

2. ______________________________

3. ______________________________

4. ______________________________

Lesson 3 Germs, germs, germs

Activity 3.3b How to wash your hands correctly

Can you write or draw step-by-step instructions to show how to wash your hands correctly?

1

2

3

4

5

6

Unit reflection

Create a poster to be displayed in your school which shows ways that we can all lead healthier lives. What can people do to stay healthy?

Unit 2.4 Feeling included

You are there when I need you,
You are there when I feel sad,
You are there when I celebrate.
Oh what fun we've had!

You like the things that I do,
Although sometimes they are not alike,
But that doesn't matter
Because we both like riding a bike.

What do you know?

- What do you think the poem is talking about?
- Do you have someone you feel this way about?

In this unit, you will:

- Explore how to be a good friend.
- Think about ways that you can include people in games.
- Work out why friendships might change and how you can speak to your friends if you have fallen out.

Lesson 1 A warm welcome

Activity 4.1a Being the new person

Have you ever been the new person in a class, a club or a group? Draw a picture of this. Draw how you felt. Who helped you in this situation?

Lesson 1 A warm welcome

Activity 4.1b Feeling left out

Think about other times when people might feel left out or excluded. How could they feel more included?

Draw why someone might feel left out in one box and how they could feel more included in the other.

Lesson 2 Including everyone

Activity 4.2a Games for everyone

Play a game with your family members that you play with your friends at school. Owing to different ages, you would have to change some things. How do you adapt it to make sure that everyone is included?

After the game is over, write or draw your ideas and observations below.

The activity

How did you adapt it?

How did people feel?

Lesson 2 Including everyone

Activity 4.2b Including others

Imagine that someone feels left out of a game.

List three things you could do to include them.

1. ______________________________

2. ______________________________

3. ______________________________

Lesson 3 We've fallen out

Activity 4.3a I feel that ...

If you fall out with a friend, it is important to be able to say how you feel. Sometimes you need time to think about this.

Think of some sentences which you can say to express how you might feel. For example, 'I feel that you aren't listening to me and it's making me upset.'

I ____________________

____

____

____

____

I ____________________

____

____

____

____

I ____________________

____

____

____

____

Lesson 3 We've fallen out

Activity 4.3b Top tips

Create a top tips leaflet to help people know what to do if they have fallen out with someone. Ask your family members for their tips too and include them here.

TOP TIPS

Unit reflection

When you think of a friend, what words do you think of?

Can you create an acrostic poem for the word 'friend'? Remember, the first word of each sentence needs to match a letter in FRIEND. Don't forget to illustrate your poem.

F

R

I

E

N

D

Unit 2.5 Being good friends

What do you know?

- What do you think is happening in each of the pictures?
- How does each person feel?
- Have you ever been in a situation like this?
- How did it make you feel?

In this unit, you will:

- Help to solve conflicts and learn how to listen and communicate carefully.
- Practise the skills needed to be an upstander by working out solutions to different bullying scenarios.
- Explore the word 'boundary' and practise phrases you can use if you feel uncomfortable.

Lesson 1 There are two sides to every story

Activity 5.1a Conflict

What is conflict? What does it mean? Draw or write all of your ideas to create a mind map below.

Can you think of any other words which mean the same as conflict?

Conflict

Lesson 1 There are two sides to every story

Activity 5.1b Possible solutions

Think of the pictures you saw two pages ago. What might the children be arguing about or why did they fall out? Can you write or draw possible solutions to the problems?

What the problems could be

Possible solutions

Lesson 2 Bullying is never OK

Activity 5.2a Being an upstander

Asha loved spending time with her friends, playing games and exploring the beautiful park near her house. She had a heart as bright as the sun, always ready to share smiles and laughter.

One sunny morning, as Asha skipped to the park, she noticed a sad look on her friend Elsie's face. Elsie was sitting on a bench, looking downcast.

Asha hurried over, "Hi, Elsie. What's wrong?" she asked.

Elsie looked up, her eyes a bit watery. She told Asha about a group of older kids who were being unkind to her at school. They were saying hurtful words and making her feel small.

Asha's heart felt heavy like a raincloud. She hugged Elsie tightly and said, "What can I do to help?"

As the days passed, Asha noticed Elsie's sparkle fading, like a dimming star. The older kids continued to tease her, and Asha knew she had to do something. She believed in the power of kindness and decided to be an upstander.

The next day at school, when the older kids started making fun of Elsie, Asha stepped forward with a determined smile. "Stop that! It's not nice to make fun of someone," she said confidently.

To her surprise, some other kids joined her too. They told the older kids that kindness was the way to go. The bullies felt outnumbered and, slowly, they stopped their hurtful actions.

Lesson 2 Bullying is never OK

Activity 5.2b Finding a solution

Think of situations where you might have seen someone be unkind the way the older kids were to Elsie in the story. How could you or someone else help solve the problem?

Think carefully about all of the ways in which people can make such situations better. You might like to share your ideas with a family member.

Draw or explain what happened.

How was the problem solved?

Lesson 3 Boundaries

Activity 5.3a Respecting boundaries

Talk to your parents/guardians about the meaning of personal space and its importance. Cut out the sentences on the page printed by your guardian. Do the sentences show someone respecting boundaries or not respecting them? Put the sentences into the correct column below.

Respects boundaries	Does not respect boundaries

Lesson 3 Boundaries

Activity 5.3b Respect my boundaries

Create a poster which shows how to respect people's boundaries. Remember to include some helpful phrases which you can say if someone is not respecting you. Don't forget to make your poster colourful and fun.

Unit reflection

Read the sentences below. If you agree with them, draw a smiley face; if you disagree, draw a sad face.

	Agree or disagree?
It's OK to watch someone being unkind to someone else.	
If you fall out with a friend, it means you can't be friends any more.	
It's OK for a friend to hold your hand even if you don't like it.	
Being an upstander means taking action when you see someone being treated in an unkind way.	
If you are angry with a friend, you should shout at them or be unkind.	

Unit 2.6 Emergency!

What do you know?

- What can you see in the picture?
- Circle any of the places in the house where you think dangers might happen.

In this unit, you will:

- Learn how to call the emergency services if you need them.
- Learn how to keep safe in the water while having fun.
- Learn how to keep safe in your home.

Lesson 1 Staying safe at home

Activity 6.1a Your home

Draw a picture of your home. You can draw a specific room or the whole house. What makes you feel safe here?

Lesson 1 Staying safe at home

Activity 6.1b Keep medicines safe

Medicines need to be stored very carefully. They can be dangerous when taken by someone they are not meant for. They can also spoil easily if they are left open. Draw a poster or picture which can remind people how to keep medicines safe. You can use words, pictures or both.

Lesson 2 What is an emergency?

Activity 6.2 Important information

When making an emergency call, it is important to know some key facts about yourself and those around you. Fill in the boxes below with your important details. Ask your family members in case there is something you cannot fill up.

My full name is ______________________________

____

My address is

House/flat name or number

____

Street or road name

____

Town or village name

____

County/state/region

____

Postcode/zip code

____

I am ______________________ years old and my date of birth is ______________________

I live with (write the full names of people who live in your home)

____

____

____

____

____

I am allergic to or have medication for

____

____

____

____

me

Lesson 3 Water safety

Activity 6.3a Fun in the water

How do you like to have fun in the water? Draw all of the ways below.

Lesson 3 Water safety

Activity 6.3b How to keep safe in the water

Research the risks which water may present, what advice you can give to people to keep safe and how they can be rescued if needed.

Unit reflection

In the space below, draw a picture showing how you would do an everyday activity safely. There are some activity suggestions below or you can come up with your own idea!

- Crossing the road
- Helping out in the kitchen
- Having medicine when you are unwell

Unit 2.7 Looking to the future

What do you know?

- What can you see in the picture?
- What do you think is happening?
- How do you think the characters feel?

In this unit, you will:

- Order the life cycle of a human.
- Create 'I can' posters to show all of the things you can do now and would like to do in the future.
- Explore how it feels to move to a different class or year group.

Lesson 1 Identifying positive changes

Activity 7.1a Positive changes

What changes do you think are positive? Draw them in the shapes below.

Lesson 1 Identifying positive changes

Activity 7.1b A letter to my future self

Write a letter to yourself which you will read in the future. Write what positive changes you are looking forward to this year in school. Think about the things you would like to achieve or do.

Dear

Lesson 2 What job would I like when I grow up?

Activity 7.2a Me at work in 20 years' time

Draw a picture of you at work in 20 years' time. What type of equipment might you need?

Lesson 2 What job would I like when I grow up?

Activity 7.2b Who am I?

Stick in photos below of you dressed up for different jobs. Or you can choose three different jobs and draw what uniform or equipment you might need for that job.

Lesson 3 It's OK to make mistakes

Activity 7.3a Marshmallow challenge!

Take all your friends or family members together and make teams of three people. Using marshmallows and spaghetti sticks, create the tallest tower that can stand by itself in fifteen minutes. Afterwards, try answering the questions below.

How did you work together?

____

____

What did you find easy?

____

____

What did you find difficult?

____

____

Was your marshmallow tower a success?

____

____

What emotions did you feel during the activity?

____

____

Lesson 3 It's OK to make mistakes

Activity 7.3b Don't give up

Find the following words in the wordsearch below.

goals	success	mistake
resilience	support	celebrate
determined	fail	

r	y	s	n	g	p	j	g	o	a	l	s	c
n	r	e	s	i	l	i	e	n	c	e	o	e
u	d	e	t	e	r	m	i	n	e	d	w	l
a	g	j	n	n	m	b	i	d	t	r	y	e
q	w	e	v	v	u	b	z	s	f	q	x	b
s	u	c	c	e	s	s	t	p	t	q	z	r
s	u	p	p	o	r	t	q	o	b	t	e	a
o	p	e	a	v	s	y	w	u	z	g	l	t
v	l	h	a	z	t	r	d	n	i	g	b	e
p	l	y	b	s	z	m	u	y	j	t	o	b
z	f	a	i	l	i	m	i	s	t	a	k	e

Unit reflection

What can you do if you make a mistake? What might help you to be successful?

Draw or write one strategy in each of the shapes below.

Unit 2.8 Our wonderful world

What do you know?

- Look at the photos. What can you see? Describe each photo and the details you see to a family member.
- How does each photo make you feel?

In this unit, you will:

- Learn what happens to rubbish and what the word 'biodegradable' means.
- Learn about the 4 Rs of recycling and work out ways that you can reduce what you use in the classroom.
- Research inspirational people in history and create a fact file.

Lesson 1 Our beautiful world

Activity 8.1 My beautiful place

Think of a beautiful place that you have visited or would like to visit which is natural (not made by people). This can be near your home or far away. Draw a picture of your beautiful place below.

Lesson 2 Reducing for the planet

Activity 8.2a What are the 4 Rs?

Look at the images below and write a sentence about each one. What does each R word mean? Take the help of the adults in your family, and check your dictionary for their definitions too.

REFUSE

REDUCE

REUSE

RECYCLE

Lesson 2 Reducing for the planet

Activity 8.2b Reducing waste in the classroom

How could your class reduce waste in your classroom? Draw or write one idea in each of the bins below.

Lesson 2 Reducing for the planet

Activity 8.2c Eco warrior wordsearch

Can you find all of the words?

climate	protect	refuse
earth	recycle	reuse
environment	reduce	world

s	g	t	w	c	r	e	u	s	e	z	n
n	q	r	a	i	p	n	d	x	e	a	v
w	m	j	l	g	r	v	s	a	l	c	p
s	w	z	y	c	l	i	m	a	t	e	r
n	c	b	e	a	o	r	e	d	u	c	e
b	r	w	l	p	r	o	t	e	c	t	f
w	a	f	x	u	o	n	p	r	b	h	u
o	s	i	y	h	e	m	k	x	q	d	s
r	e	c	y	c	l	e	a	r	t	h	e
l	b	n	c	e	s	n	g	i	p	w	a
d	m	w	q	x	a	t	g	d	j	e	l

Lesson 3 Celebrating people who made a difference

Activity 8.3a I would most like to be remembered for ...

What things are important to you? What would you like to be known for? Some examples might be your kindness, inventions, problem-solving, standing up for people. Write three things you would like to be known for below.

1.

2.

3.

Lesson 3 Celebrating people who made a difference

Activity 8.3b My inspirational fact file

Is there a person from the past that you idolize or consider your hero? Write about them and what made them heroic below.

Name:

When they were born:

Where they were born:

When they died:

What was their job?

What did they do that was inspirational?

Unit reflection

Write or draw three things which you have learned from this unit.

1.

2.

3.

What one change can you make to help the environment?

Wellbeing for kids

Making kids smarter, happier

STAGE 3

Hello and welcome to Wellbeing Stage 3!

Let's have a look at some of the things we will be learning about in this book.
It's very exciting!

Emotions

We are going to take a look at lots of different feelings and why it helps to talk about them.

Health

We are also going to explore lots of ways to take care of ourselves in our body and our mind so that we feel amazing.

Families

We will look at lots of different types of families, think about what love means and why kindness is important.

Listen up

We'll take a look at how to be a good listener and how to stand up for yourself when you need to.

Safety

Keeping yourself safe is very important, so we are going to look at following rules and who to ask for help when we need it.

Changes

Life is full of changes and changes can be fun, but sometimes they can feel a bit scary. In this section, we are going to practise how to cope with new things more easily.

The whole wide world

And finally, it's important to think about other people too and realise we are very much the same but also very different. You will see what I mean as we head to the end of the book.

There are so many cool things to learn and discover, about helping yourself, other people and the planet.

Shall we make a start?

May your year be as delightful as YOU!

Becky Goddard-Hill

Unit 3.1 My emotions and feelings

What do you know?

- What can you see in the pictures?
- Have you ever experienced what is happening in the pictures?
- Share your experiences with a friend.

In this unit, you will:

- Explore how feeling scared can make our bodies react and how we can stop ourselves from feeling so scared.
- Consider how people feel when they have lost something.
- Play spot the difference games.

Lesson 1 I feel scared

Activity 1.1a Lily and the thunderstorm

1. Look at the images above and think about what's happening with Lily. Why does she feel scared?

2. What could Lily do to make herself feel less scared? Draw or write your answer below.

Lesson 1 I feel scared

Activity 1.1b When I feel scared

Think of the things you can do to make yourself feel calmer when you feel worried or scared.

Draw your ideas in the bubbles below.

Lesson 1 I feel scared

Activity 1.1c What happens to my body when I am scared?

On the body below, label things which happen to our body when we are scared.

Lesson 2 Loss

Activity 1.2a Alara and Teddy

Alara is a young girl who is very fond of her stuffed teddy bear. She carries it everywhere with her, whether it is to school or the park. One afternoon, she returns home and opens her school bag to find Teddy missing. Alara is sad, and with her parents' help, she creates posters to help find Teddy, pasting them all over her neighbourhood and school.

Can you create illustrations to show what has happened in the story? Think carefully about the main points in the story. What do you think might have happened next?

How did Alara feel at each stage of the story?

1. ______________________________

2. ______________________________

3. ______________________________

4. ______________________________

5. ______________________________

Lesson 2 Loss

Activity 1.2b Spot the difference

Can you spot the differences? Circle the differences you can see and colour in the pictures.

Unit reflection

Share with your family members three things you have learned from this unit. Write or draw them in the boxes below. Think carefully about how your body reacts to emotions, how you manage big emotions and how you feel about loss.

Unit 3.2 Managing my big emotions

What do you know?

- What are the people in the picture doing?
- How do you know? What clues are there?

In this unit, you will:

- Identify people you trust to talk to.
- Explore different ways to deal with big feelings.
- Try out some different relaxation techniques.

Lesson 1 Talking is good

Activity 2.1a Who can you talk to?

Think of four people that you can talk to about any problems you might have. Write their names below.

Lesson 1 Talking is good

Activity 2.1b Big emotions wordsearch

Can you find these big emotion words?

joyous	hopeful	embarrassed	scared	happy
frustrated	sad	worried	angry	excited

t	e	m	b	a	r	r	a	s	s	e	d
e	x	u	r	t	i	b	w	c	a	t	a
g	c	m	k	p	r	u	b	a	d	k	e
n	i	s	c	j	w	o	r	r	i	e	d
d	t	f	z	o	i	r	n	e	g	p	h
q	e	a	g	y	s	f	j	d	f	q	a
y	d	n	h	o	p	e	f	u	l	g	p
h	z	g	l	u	c	j	m	i	z	o	p
e	f	r	u	s	t	r	a	t	e	d	y
t	c	y	l	o	s	f	z	y	c	n	o

Lesson 2 Jealousy

Activity 2.2a I feel jealous

Draw or write about a time when you have felt jealous. Why do you think you felt like this?

I felt jealous when

Lesson 2 Jealousy

Activity 2.2b What is jealousy?

Jealousy can make us feel like we are losing out in a competition for affection or in achievement.

When we feel jealous, we can also feel a bit anxious and that is because our stress hormones are in overdrive. We might also feel a bit achy as being jealous activates the part of the brain that processes physical pain.

Read the text with a friend or in a group and write your own definition of jealousy. What does it mean?

Lesson 2 Jealousy

Activity 2.2c Create a monster

What do you think jealousy would look like as a monster? What colour might it be? What would its body and face look like?

Lesson 3 Learning to relax

Activity 2.3 Relaxation activities

Have you heard of the term 'self-care'? It means taking care of ourselves physically, mentally and emotionally to feel good. It is very important to prioritise self-care in our daily lives. With the help of your parents/guardians engage in a few self-care activities like yoga, dancing or sketching. As you take part in each activity, think about how it makes you feel. What did you enjoy about each one? Did you have a favourite?

Activity one – kids' yoga

Activity two – colouring

Activity three – singing

Unit reflection

Think about the things you have learned about in this unit. Read the comments below and decide if you agree or disagree with them. Put a tick in the agree box or the disagree box.

	Agree	Disagree
It is important to talk about your feelings.		
Being jealous is a normal emotion.		
It is important that we find strategies which can help to calm our minds and relax us.		
Everybody uses the same strategies to relax.		
People can act in different ways because of their emotions.		
Remembering your own strengths can help you when you feel jealous.		

Unit 3.3 Taking care of myself

What do you know?

- What can you see in the photo?
- How does the photo make you feel?
- Can you think of a time when you did something similar?

In this unit, you will:

- Spend some time outside and consider how it makes you feel.
- Create an allergy-friendly recipe book.
- Work out a bedtime routine which will help you get to sleep.
- Explore different ways to rest and which ones suit you best.

Lesson 1 Spending time outside

Activity 3.1a Nature sketch

With an adult, visit your local park or garden. Choose a natural object and look closely at it. What shape is it? What colours can you see? Are there any patterns?

Carefully sketch your nature object below.

Lesson 1 Spending time outside

Activity 3.1b Nature scavenger hunt

Here's a list of things that are found outdoors. Can you find all of the items on the list? Write what you are looking for in the table below and tick when you have found it. Be careful while outdoors and do not handle objects without adult supervision.

Item	Did you find it?
A leaf	
A smooth pebble	
A flower	
A berry	
A small twig	
A blade of grass	
The bark of a tree	

Draw a picture below of your favourite object from the scavenger hunt.

Lesson 2 What are allergies?

Activity 3.2a Allergies

Allergies are a reaction of our body's immune system to certain substances, called allergens, which can be found in foods, the environment or even on animals. Some are common, like pollen or peanuts, while others are not. Go online with a trusted adult and find out about various common allergies, and what precautions one should take while eating with each of them.

Can eat	Should not eat

Lesson 2 What are allergies?

Activity 3.2b Our allergy friendly recipe

As you find out more about the different kinds of allergies and how they can make people very unwell, try finding out foods and ingredients that people with any of the allergies you have researched can eat without problems. Then, using those ingredients, create an allergy friendly recipe! Take the help of an adult for this.

RECIPE

TITLE: ____________________

____________________ PREP TIME

____________________ TOTAL TIME

INGREDIENTS

____________________ ____________________

____________________ ____________________

____________________ ____________________

WHAT TO DO

____

____

____

____

____

____

Lesson 3 Sleep and rest

Activity 3.3a My bedtime routine

Think of the things you do to help you get to sleep. What does your bedtime routine look like?

Lesson 3 Sleep and rest

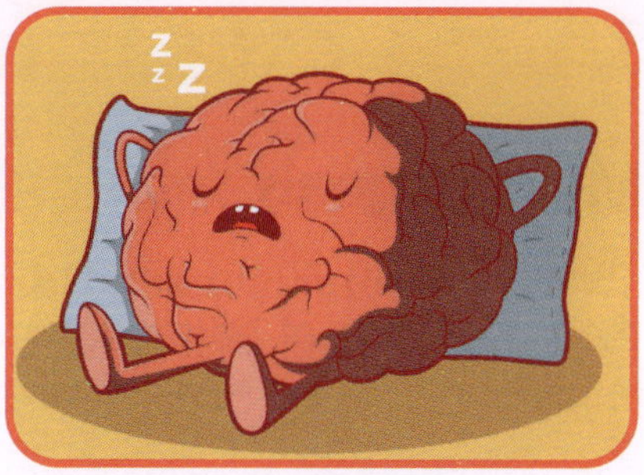

Activity 3.3b Types of rest

Rest is a way of giving our bodies a little break. It helps us feel less tired, calmer and ready to play again. It's like taking a deep breath for our bodies. Create a poster below of all the ways you can rest your body or mind.

Unit reflection

My rest goals

Think carefully about all the things you have learned about in this unit: the importance of being outside, how to create recipes which everyone can enjoy and why we need to sleep and rest.

Can you think of any goals which you could set to lead an even healthier life? Think of what you might need to do to achieve this goal.

My goal is ______________________________

____

____

I can achieve this by ______________________________

____

____

____

Unit 3.4 Kindness and love

> NO ACT OF KINDNESS, NO MATTER HOW SMALL, IS EVER WASTED.
>
> Aesop

What do you know?

- What do you think the quote from Aesop means?
- Think of a time when you have been kind.
- What acts of kindness do you show your family or friends?

In this unit, you will:

- Explore ways that you can make a difference to people.
- Create paper plate puppets of your family.
- Create a class book about how families are different.

Lesson 1 I can help make a difference

Activity 4.1a Social responsibility

What is social responsibility? Caring about other people and about the world we live in is being socially responsible. We need to consider how our personal choices affect others and the wider world. Discuss this with the adults in your family and then write a definition for social responsibility in your own words. You can illustrate your definition with example pictures.

Social responsibility means ______________________________

Lesson 1 I can help make a difference

Activity 4.1b Freeze-frame guessing game

Draw pictures to show acts of service and write how the act is about social responsibility.

Lesson 1 I can help make a difference

Activity 4.1c My pledge

Pledge one way in which you can spread happiness and kindness in your home, school and community. Discuss it with your family members and encourage your friends to do the same. Write your pledge below and draw a picture of it.

My pledge is ______________________________

____

____

____

____

Lesson 2 What is a family?

Activity 4.2a Different families

Think of what family means to you. What words or ideas do you think of when you hear the word 'family'?

Write some sentences below.

Family is ______________________

Family is ______________________

Family is ______________________

Lesson 2 What is a family?

Activity 4.2b What is special about my family?

Think what makes your family special. Write or draw your ideas, or do both. Ask your family members to join in the activity too.

Lesson 3 Families are the same and different

Activity 4.3 Different and the same

Think of ways in which families are different and the same. Draw and write your ideas below. For example, some families are big, some families are small, but all families like to celebrate special days. Don't forget to illustrate your page. Copy the page and give a copy to each of your friends, asking them to fill theirs. The pages can then be put together to make a book of families.

Some families have ______________________________

____

____

But all families ______________________________

____

____

Unit reflection

In this unit you have learned that families can look different, celebrate different things and have different traditions, which is what makes them so great, as well as how important social responsibility is.

Draw a picture of things you do which make friends and others happy. How do you help them?

Unit 3.5 Sharing time with people around me

What do you know?

- What is happening in each photo?
- Why is this important?
- Can you think of any other examples?

In this unit, you will:

- Practise active listening and discover why it is so important.
- Create a family activity jar.
- Explore different scenarios and discuss how you can encourage people.
- Identify ways in which you might be pressured and how you can say 'No, thank you' if you don't feel comfortable.

Lesson 1 How do you spend time with family?

Activity 5.1a How do you feel?

How do you feel when you spend time with your family or loved ones? Write down your emotion words in the space below. You can draw emojis and label them or write the words.

Lesson 1 How do you spend time with family?

Activity 5.1b Family time

Write or draw three things you like to do with your family or loved ones. How do they make you feel?

1. ______________________________

____

2. ______________________________

____

3. ______________________________

____

Lesson 2 What is good listening?

Activity 5.2a What are active listening skills?

Active listening means being completely engaged in a conversation. When a person wants to know what happened and understand what another is saying, rather than just trying to speak what they want to, it means they are actively listening. What would you see or feel if someone is actively listening to you?

Lesson 2 What is good listening?

Activity 5.2b Being a good listener

We know it is important to listen carefully to others, but why?

How do you think being a good listener will help you in your school life, home life and in the future? Draw or write some ways below.

Lesson 3 Be encouraging

Activity 5.3a Wordsearch

Can you find all the key words in the wordsearch?

friend	praise	encourage	feelings	positive
support	push	choice	pressure	decision

w	p	r	a	i	s	e	h	j
h	u	c	i	d	u	p	n	l
f	s	h	f	q	p	r	p	l
r	h	o	a	a	p	j	y	f
i	c	i	p	k	o	m	b	e
e	n	c	o	u	r	a	g	e
n	b	e	s	z	t	r	e	l
d	w	n	i	u	v	s	t	i
s	j	q	t	k	t	l	h	n
d	e	c	i	s	i	o	n	g
a	v	g	v	u	r	q	p	s
d	p	r	e	s	s	u	r	e

Lesson 3 Be encouraging

Activity 5.3b What would you do?

Your classmates are teasing another student because they're wearing different clothes. They want you to join in and make fun of them. What would you do?

Unit reflection

Why is it important to spend time with our families or people we love?

____

____

____

How could you improve your listening skills?

____

____

____

How could you be more encouraging and supportive of the people you love or enjoy spending time with?

____

____

____

Unit 3.6 How can I keep myself safe?

What do you know?

- Look at the photos.
  - What do you like to do in sunny weather?
  - Have you ever seen snow?
  - What do you like to do in cold weather?
  - Which is your favourite?

In this unit, you will:

- Learn how to keep safe in the sun.
- Explore the ways to keep safe when you are on your computer or devices.

Lesson 1 Staying safe in different weathers

Activity 6.1 Staying safe in the sun

Circle the things that can keep you safe in the sun.

What other things can you think of?

____

____

____

____

Lesson 2 Keeping myself safe

Activity 6.2a What could they do?

A boy in his class keeps pushing Lee in the playground. He doesn't like it. He feels uncomfortable.

What could Lee say? Write what he could say below and practise this phrase.

What should Sara do?

Her mum's friend keeps sitting really close to Sara. She doesn't like it. She feels uncomfortable.

Write what she could say or do below.

Lesson 2 Keeping myself safe

Activity 6.2b Who are my trusted adults?

Write someone you trust on each finger of the hand.

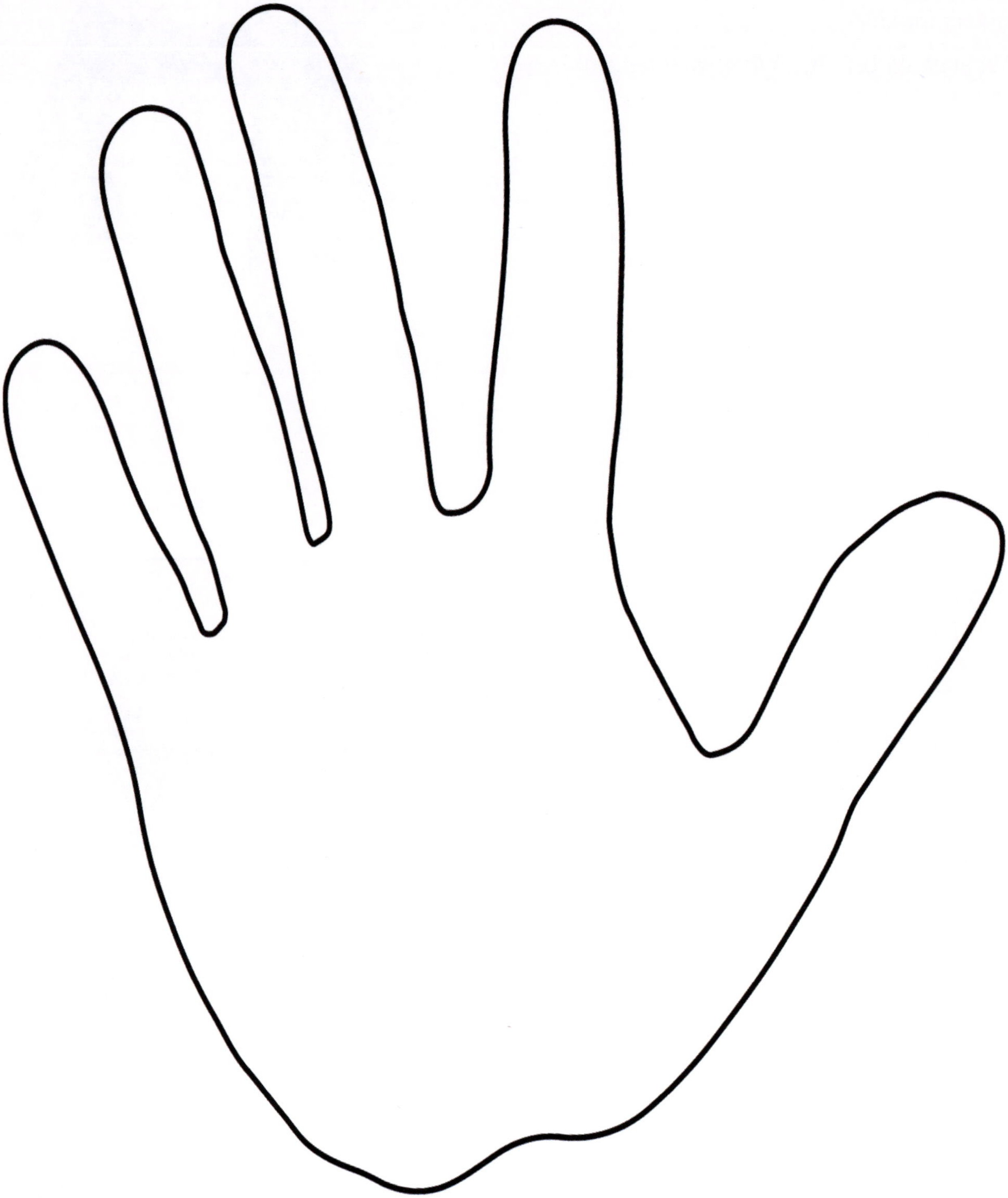

Lesson 2 Keeping myself safe

Activity 6.2c Who helps me in school?

Draw and write the names of the adults in school who you can talk to if you need help. Draw and write the names of the adults in school who are safeguarding leads.

Lesson 3 Do I know you?

Activity 6.3a Rahim at the park

Rahim is at an amusement park with his mother and sister. The place is full of people and all sorts of attractions that Rahim wants to try out. But his mother is urging Rahim to slow down as she is carrying his sister too. Rahim then spots a water slide he really wants to try. In his excitement, he runs towards it, only to turn around and see that he can't find his mother or his sister. He goes back to where he last saw them, but they aren't there.

Now, answer the questions below. What do you think happens next?

What should Rahim do when he can't see his mum?

____

____

____

What did Rahim do that was wrong?

____

____

____

Lesson 3 Do I know you?

Activity 6.3b Safer strangers

Look at the clues. Who do you think they are describing? Draw the person.

	This person helps to keep the law. They make sure that everyone is safe from crime and harm.
	This person teaches you lots of things in school.
	This person works in a place where you can buy things.

Who would you go to for help if you were lost?

Unit reflection

If you are ever in a situation where you don't feel safe, what could you do? Think how you could keep safe in different weather. Write your ideas in the shapes.

SAFETY FIRST

Unit 3.7 Growing and learning

What do you know?

- What can you see in the picture?
- What do you think the picture means?
- How do you think the person playing this game or sport might be feeling?

In this unit, you will:

- Explore the ways you learn best.
- Create some scribble animals and a resilience poster or leaflet.
- Consider ways in which we can prepare for change.

Lesson 1 How do I learn?

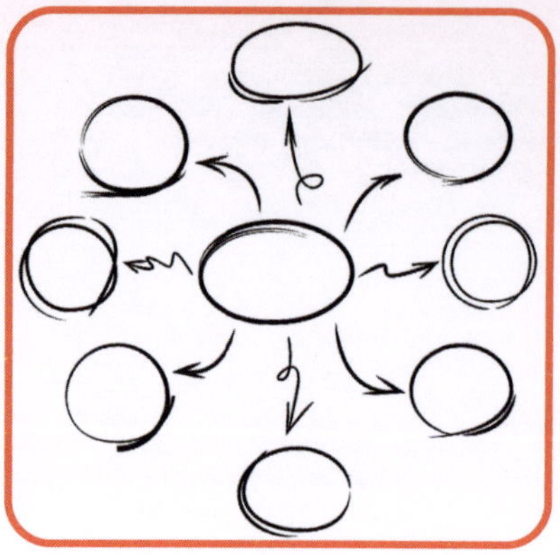

Activity 7.1a What did I learn?

Watch a video about the solar system by the Free School channel on YouTube. After watching the video, can you create a mind map, picture or other visually creative way of showing what you learned?

Lesson 1 How do I learn?

Activity 7.1b What helps you to learn?

Think about how you like to learn. Do you like to learn in a group or on your own? Do questions help you to understand? What strategies work best for you?

Draw some pictures of the best ways for you to learn.

Lesson 2 It's OK to fail

Activity 7.2a Animal scribbles

Create a scribble in the frame below. Then see if you can change your scribble into an animal picture.

Lesson 2 It's OK to fail

Activity 7.2b Resilience poster

Can you create an advice poster which shows how people can be more resilient when they find something difficult. Think of all the useful ways that could help when people feel like giving up.

Make your poster as interesting, colourful and informative as you can so that this can be shared with other classes in your school.

Lesson 3 When change feels a little scary

Activity 7.3a What would you do?

Man-Yee's parents have moved to a different country, taking her with them. She's new to your school, and looks scared as it is nothing like her previous school. Imagine you saw Man-Yee in the playground of your school alone. What would you do?

Around the picture, draw or write some examples of things you would do or say to make Man-Yee feel less alone.

Lesson 3 When change feels a little scary

Activity 7.3b A scary feeling

Draw a picture depicting a change or situation that you found scary, for example when you moved schools or countries, when you started a new club, when your baby brother or sister was born. Write words or phrases describing how you felt about the change.

Unit reflection

In this unit you have been learning that it is OK to make mistakes and that mistakes can make us more resilient. You have also been learning that sometimes change might feel scary, but there are lots of ways we can make it manageable.

Imagine you are a rubber ball. Draw a picture of your face in the ball shape below.

Around the ball, write or draw three things you can do to help you bounce back when you make a mistake.

Unit 3.8 Rights and respect for our world

What do you know?

- Look at the picture.
- What can you see?
- What facts do you know about the world?

In this unit, you will:

- Explore what rights are and create a class charter.
- Explore ways to save water and find out why water is so important for our world.
- Go on a nature walk and find out what lives in your local area.

Lesson 1 Rights for all

Activity 8.1 What are rights?

What are rights?

Lesson 2 Looking after our world's water

Activity 8.2a How do you use water every day?

Write or draw the ways you or your family uses water every day.

Lesson 2 Looking after our world's water

Activity 8.2b I am a water warrior

Even though over 70% of our planet is full of water, we can only use a tiny fraction of it for our daily use. Fresh water, therefore, is a rare resource and needs to be saved and not wasted. Talk to your elders about the importance of water and how water wastage can happen. Find out what you can do to help and pledge to be a water warrior below.

I pledge that I will ____________________

____

____

____

____

____

____

____

____

____

____

____

____________________ *to help save water.*

Lesson 2 Looking after our world's water

Activity 8.2c Water warriors quiz

Can you answer these questions? Put a circle around the correct answer.

1. What can you do to save water in the garden?
   a) Use a big hose all the time.
   b) Water the plants in the dark.
   c) Collect rainwater for the plants.

2. How is it best to wash your car?
   a) Use a bucket of water.
   b) Use a hose.
   c) Put the car under a waterfall.

3. How can you save water when you take a bath?
   a) Fill the tub all the way to the top.
   b) Splash a lot in the tub.
   c) Fill the tub halfway.

4. How can you help keep water clean?
   a) Throw rubbish in the rivers or oceans.
   b) Use lots of chemicals near water.
   c) Put rubbish in the right place and don't make water dirty.

5. When you brush your teeth you should:
   a) Keep the tap running.
   b) Turn off the tap.
   c) Fill the bath.

Lesson 3 Who really lives in your local area?

Activity 8.3a Who do you think lives here?

Draw or write what or who you think lives in your neighbourhood. Look at the picture your parent/guardian shows you.

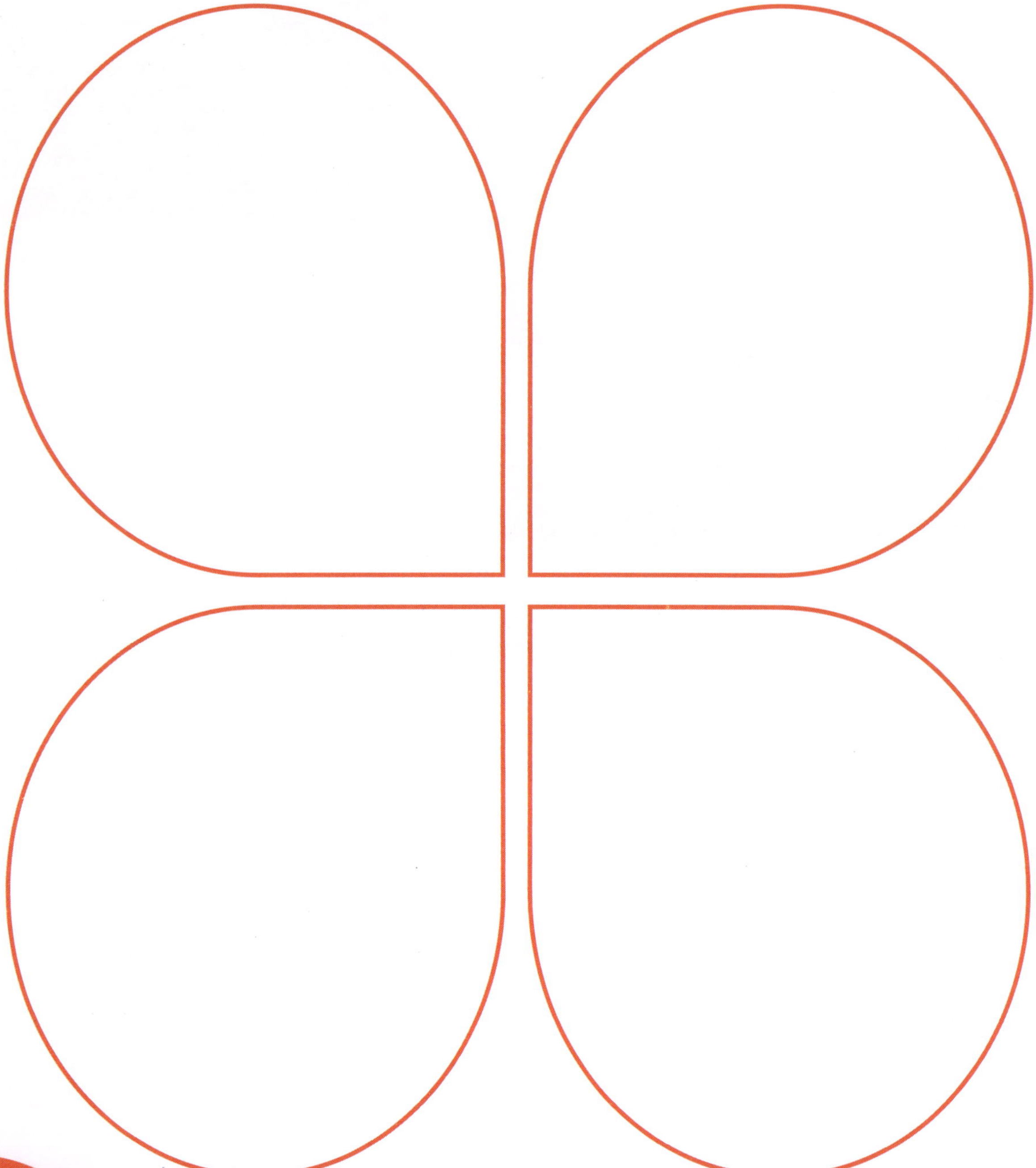

Lesson 3 Who really lives in your local area?

Activity 8.3b What did you find on your investigation?

Create a tally chart of the types of creatures or animals you found. Be sure to maintain your distance and not to disturb them while doing so.

Creature or animal	Tally
Dogs	
Cats	
Cows	
Parakeets/Parrots	
Squirrels	
Horses/Camels	

Can you create a pictogram or bar chart of the creatures or animals you found?

Unit reflection

Create an acrostic poem about our wonderful world! You can think about words to do with sustainability, saving water or rights. Your poem can use words or full sentences. Don't forget to illustrate your poem.

E

A

R

T

H

Acknowledgements

We are grateful to the following for permission to reproduce copyright material:

1.4. The poem "I'm Glad I'm Me" by Jack Prelutsky, as published in I'm glad I'm me – poems about you, Scholastic, 2006, copyright © Jack Prelutsky, 2006. Reproduced by kind permission of the author. Hello Feelings, Poppy O'Neill, illustrated by Ceej Rowland Reprinted by permission of HarperCollins Publishers Ltd © 2022 **3.2** Big Feelings, Becky Goddard-Hill, Reprinted by permission of HarperCollins Publishers Ltd © 2023 **3.7.** Man-Yee and the New School, Mio Debnam, Illustrated by Wendy Tan Shiau Wei Reprinted by permission of HarperCollins Publishers Ltd © 2021 **1.1.1** Rawpixel.com/Shutterstock, cougarsan/Shutterstock, ober-art/Shutterstock, KVASVECTOR/Shutterstock, WS **1.1.1** AyselDesign/Shutterstock, **1.1.2** WS from My Life – Early Years Foundation Stage Primary PSHE Handbook © HarperCollins Publishers 2022, BNP Design **1.1.3** Monkey Business Images/ Shutterstock, pakww/Shutterstock, Krakenimages. com/Shutterstock, aslysun/Shutterstock, **1.2.1** Wise ant/Shutterstock, stevemart/Shutterstock, **1.2.2** from My Life – Early Years Foundation Stage Primary PSHE Handbook © HarperCollins Publishers 2022, WS **1.2.2** from My Life – Early Years Foundation Stage Primary PSHE Handbook © HarperCollins Publishers 2022, **1.2.3** ma_nud_sen/Shutterstock, ect/Shutterstock, 1.3.1 Nungning20/Shutterstock, Natalia Lisovskaya/Shutterstock, Tatjana Baibakova/Shutterstock, Suradech Prapairat/Shutterstock, Pavel K/Shutterstock, WS **1.3.1** curiosity/Shutterstock, New Africa/Shutterstock, Nik Merkulov/Shutterstock, monticello/Shutterstock, guy42/Shutterstock, Bukhta Yurii/Shutterstock, PixaHub/Shutterstock, CWIS/Shutterstock, New Africa/Shutterstock, Nasir hameed siddiqui/Shutterstock, andersphoto/Shutterstock, Alter-ego/Shutterstock, Photoongraphy/Shutterstock, studiovin/Shutterstock, WIPHARAT CHAINUPAPHA/Shutterstock, ilolab/Shutterstock, Designs Stock/Shutterstock, Spalnic/Shutterstock, Maks Narodenko/Shutterstock, Charles Brutlag/Shutterstock, baibaz/Shutterstock, Val_R/Shutterstock, Pixel-Shot/Shutterstock, spaxiax/Shutterstock, 1.3.3 WS 1.3.3a from My Life – Early Years Foundation Stage Primary PSHE Handbook © HarperCollins Publishers 2022, WS 1.3.3b (tl) BadaL_studio/Shutterstock, WS 1.3.3b (tr) Maksym Drozd/Shutterstock, WS 1.3.3b (b) Sanit Fuangnakhon/Shutterstock, Tatjana Baibakova/Shutterstock, Nadiyka U/Shutterstock, Tukunen/Shutterstock, **1.4.1** mixcolours/Shutterstock, **1.4.2** WS 1.4.2 BlueRingMedia/Shutterstock, Aleksandr_Lysenko/Shutterstock, 1.4.2 WS 1.4.2 from My Life – Early Years Foundation Stage Primary PSHE Handbook © HarperCollins Publishers 2022, WS 1.4.3 from My Life – Early Years Foundation Stage Primary PSHE Handbook © HarperCollins Publishers 202, Tenstudio/ Shutterstock, **1.5.1** WS 1.5.1a from My Life – Early Years Foundation Stage Primary PSHE Handbook © HarperCollins Publishers 2022, Monkey Business Images/ Shutterstock,**1.5.3** WS 1.5.3 from My Life – Early Years Foundation Stage Primary PSHE Handbook © HarperCollins Publishers 2022, Olga1818/Shutterstock, BNP Design Studio/Shutterstock, Andrey_Kuzmin/Shutterstock, lineartestpilot/Shutterstock, **1.6.1** Bonezboyz/Shutterstock, stevemart/Shutterstock, **1.6.3** Carkhe/Shutterstock, Lemberg Vector studio/Shutterstock, pavla/Shutterstock, BNP Design Studio/Shutterstock, William Perugini/Shutterstock, New Africa/Shutterstock, **1.7.1** GoodStudio/Shutterstock, WS 1.7.1 GoodStudio/Shutterstock, Lemonade Serenade/ Shutterstock, **1.7.3** Prostock-studio/Shutterstock, My Life – Early Years Foundation Stage Primary PSHE Handbook © HarperCollins Publishers 2022, 1.8.1 Oksana Mizina/Shutterstock, beats1/Shutterstock, Losangela/Shutterstock, Tatjana Baibakova/Shutterstock, BestForBest/Shutterstock, Aedka Studio/Shutterstock, noBorders – Brayden Howie/Shutterstock, Chad Zuber/Shutterstock, Maria_Ermolenko/Shutterstock, WS 1.8.1 BestForBest/Shutterstock, Aedka Studio/Shutterstock, noBorders – Brayden Howie/Shutterstock, Chad Zuber/Shutterstock, Maria_Ermolenko/Shutterstock, Its design/Shutterstock, **1.8.2** galaira/Shutterstock, Wise ant/Shutterstock, **1.8.3** BNP Design Studio/Shutterstock, Ruth Black/Shutterstock, Dina Saeed/Shutterstock, WS 1.8.3a stockvit/ Shutterstock, Pro Symbols/ Shutterstock, Viktorija Reuta/ Shutterstock, Warmworld/ Adobe stock, Tassia_K/ Shutterstock, EPS/ Shutterstock. **2.1.1** Katerina Davidenko/Shutterstock, Wat cartoon/Shutterstock, KanKhem/Shutterstock, **2.1.2** My Life – Key Stage 1 Primary PSHE Handbook © HarperCollins Publishers 2022, **2.1.3** Hakase_420/Shutterstock, PeopleImages.com – Yuri A/Shutterstock, WS 2.1.3 Hakase_420/Shutterstock, PeopleImages.com – Yuri A/Shutterstock, **2.2.1** yusufdemirci/Shutterstock, Shysheep/Shutterstock, **2.2.2** WS 2.2.2 ANNA ZASIMOVA/Shutterstock, **2.3.1** Wanwisspaul/Shutterstock, **2.3.2** yut548/Shutterstock, **2.3.3** BNP Design Studio/Shutterstock, girafchik/Shutterstock, **2.4.2** mixcolours/ Shutterstock, TinnaPong/Shutterstock, **2.4 3** Colorfuel Studio/Shutterstock, tanyabosyk/Shutterstock, **2.5 1** Tartila/ Shutterstock, **2.5.2** WindAwake/ Shutterstock, **2.6 1** GoodStudio/Shutterstock, stevemart/Shutterstock, **2.6 2** WikaGraphic/Shutterstock, WS 2.6.2 WikaGraphic/Shutterstock, 3d Jesus/Shutterstock, 3d Jesus/Shutterstock, **2.6.3** Prostock-studio/Shutterstock, sutadimages/Shutterstock, Evgeny Atamanenko/Shutterstock, Zhuravlev Andrey/Shutterstock, **2.7 1** ayelet-keshet/Shutterstock, Art Alex/Shutterstock, **2.7.2** AlexHliv/Shutterstock, **2.8 1** Yakov Oskanov/Shutterstock, Dmitry Rukhlenko/Shutterstock, Yakov Oskanov/Shutterstock, BGSmith/ Shutterstock, NatSarunyoo536/Shutterstock, **2.8.2** spiral media/Shutterstock, WS 2.8.2 spiral media/Shutterstock, Guilhem Menard/Shutterstock, **2.8 3** Icons Home/Shutterstock, **3.1.1** Iconic Bestiary/Shutterstock, Julia Soul Art/Shutterstock, logistock/Shutterstock, **3.2.1** Sharma/Shutterstock, Ken Vail, **3.2.2** New Africa/Shutterstock, **3.2.3** WS 3.2.3a Christina Designs/Shutterstock, WS 3.2.3b Christina Designs/Shutterstock, **3.3.1** A3pfamily/Shutterstock, Realstockvector/Shutterstock, **3.3.2** reddish/Shutterstock, **3.3.3** pedrorsfernandes/Shutterstock, **3.4.1** Devotion/Shutterstock, Emilia Dragomir/Shutterstock, WS 3.4.1 Emilia Dragomir/Shutterstock, **3.5.1** pathdoc/Shutterstock, Anna Kraynova/Shutterstock, Ground Picture/Shutterstock, ZeinousGDS/Shutterstock, **3.5.2** Vitalii Vodolazskyi/Shutterstock, iQoncept/Shutterstock, **3.5.3** Prostock-studio/Shutterstock, **3.6.1** Jacob_09/Shutterstock, paulista/Shutterstock, Efi mova Anna/Shutterstock, SB p. 42 & WS 3.6.1 Dmitry Naumov/Shutterstock, The_Molostock/Shutterstock, Maidannikov/Shutterstock, SB p. 42 & WS 3.6.1 siridhata/Shutterstock, Vitaly Titov/Shutterstock, GinaVector/Shutterstock, SB p. 42 & WS 3.6.1 Anastasia Samorodova/Shutterstock, **3.6.2** My Life – Key Stage 1 Primary PSHE Handbook © HarperCollins Publishers 2022, o_m/Shutterstock, WS 3.6.2 o_m/Shutterstock, **3.6.3** Bojani/Shutterstock, Krisztian/Shutterstock, **3.7.1** GoodStudio/Shutterstock, phipatbig/Shutterstock, WS 3.7.1 phipatbig/Shutterstock, **3.7.2** v_kulieva/Shutterstock, **3.7.3** Vasilyeva Elada/Shutterstock, OlgaKlyushina/Shutterstock, **3.8.1** max dallocco/Shutterstock, **3.8.2** Mallinka1/Shutterstock, WS 3.8.2 Mallinka1/Shutterstock, Hari_Aprianto/Shutterstock, New Africa/Shutterstock, Roman Zaiets/Shutterstock, TaraPatta/Shutterstock,

All additional text reprinted by permission of HarperCollins Publishers Ltd © 2024.

The Wellbeing for Kids Series